COUNTRY · EXPLORERS

A Visit to

COLOMBIA

By Charis Mather

BEARPORT
PUBLISHING

Minneapolis, Minnesota

Credits

All images are courtesy of Shutterstock.com, unless otherwise specified. With thanks to Getty Images, Thinkstock Photo, and iStockphoto.

Cover – Andrey Gontare, MARTINVASQUEZPHOTO. 2–3 – lemaret pierrick. 4–5 – Mikadun, Matis75. 6–7 – QQ7, Alejandro Tejada. 8–9 – MatthieuCattin, mehdi33300, Watch The World. 10–11 – Luis Echeverri Urrea, Matyas Rehak. 12–13 – doleesi, Orchid photho. 14–15 – Exequiel Schvartz, Andres Navia Paz. 16–17 – Dronoptera, Joerg Steber. 18–19 – WILLIAM RG, EGT-1. 20–21 – hillsn_1992, mehdi33300. 22–23 – Pedro Szekely, reisegraf.ch.

Library of Congress Cataloging-in-Publication Data is available at www.loc.gov or upon request from the publisher.

ISBN: 979-8-88509-974-5 (hardcover)
ISBN: 979-8-88822-153-2 (paperback)
ISBN: 979-8-88822-294-2 (ebook)

© 2024 BookLife Publishing
This edition is published by arrangement with BookLife Publishing.

CONTENTS

COUNTRY TO COUNTRY

Which country do you live in?

A country is an area of land marked by **borders**. The people in each country have their own rules and ways of living. They may speak different languages.

Each country around the world has its own interesting things to see and do. Let's take a trip to visit a country and learn more!

Have you ever visited another country?

TODAY'S TRIP IS TO
COLOMBIA!

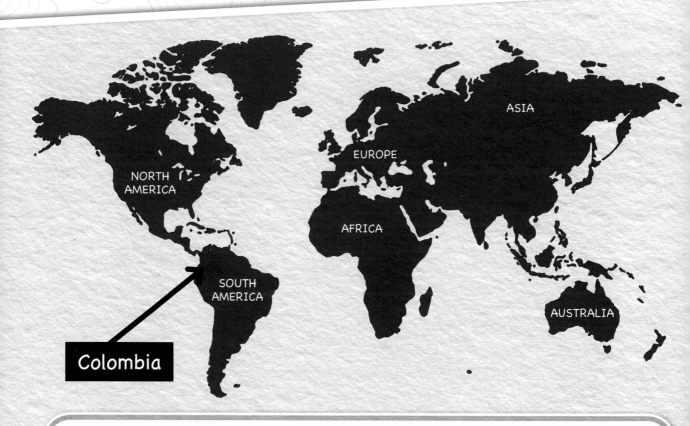

Colombia

NORTH
AMERICA

SOUTH
AMERICA

EUROPE

ASIA

AFRICA

AUSTRALIA

Colombia is a country in the **continent** of South America.

FACT FILE

Capital city: Bogotá
Main language: Spanish
Currency: Colombian peso
Flag:

Currency is the type of money that is used in a country.

BOGOTÁ

We'll start our trip in Bogotá, the capital city of Colombia. There is a mountain called Monserrate next to the city. It has a building at its top. We can see it from many parts of the city.

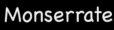

Monserrate

La Candelaria

La Candelaria is a part of Bogotá with many old and colorful buildings. We will see some amazing **street art** painted on the buildings.

9

FOOD

Bandeja paisa is the **national** dish of Colombia. It usually has beans, avocado, meat, and corn cakes called arepas. All the different foods are served on one large plate.

We could try a popular snack called chocolate caliente con queso. This is hot chocolate with cheese melted in it. First, we drink the hot chocolate. Then, we can use a spoon to eat the gooey cheese at the bottom.

BARRANQUILLA CARNIVAL

Carnival dancers

Every year, many people get together for a huge celebration called Barranquilla **Carnival**. This is one of the biggest carnivals in the world and lasts four whole days.

There is music, dancing, and shows. Many people wear colorful **costumes** and masks to celebrate. Cars drive through the streets covered in hundreds of bright flowers.

COCORA VALLEY

Let's stop by the beautiful Cocora Valley, where some of the world's tallest palm trees grow. Some of the area's wax palms can be more than 200 feet (60 m) tall.

Wax palms can live about 200 years.

While some people come to see the wax palms and the beautiful sights, others come to Cocora Valley to try Colombia's famous coffee. The area is known for growing good coffee beans.

Colombian coffee is sold all around the world.

LOST CITY

Deep in a different Colombian **jungle**, we can find an incredible lost city. **Indigenous** Colombian people built it more than 1,000 years ago.

The Lost City was built into the side of a mountain. It had different levels, each with homes and gathering places. The Lost City once had more than 2,000 people living there.

There are 1,200 stone steps that go up to the city.

WAYUU PEOPLE

The Wayuu is one of the largest groups of indigenous peoples in Colombia. Many live in Colombia's biggest desert, La Guajira. Wayuu houses are often made with dried cacti and palm leaves.

Some Wayuu people **weave** beautiful bags and hammocks by hand. In Wayuu stories, people were taught how to weave by a spider called Walekeru.

GUATAPÉ

Ready for a climb? Let's take the long staircase up the side of a huge rock that sticks out of the ground near the town of Guatapé. The rock is about 650 ft (200 m) tall.

After getting down from the climb, we can wander around Guatapé's bright and colorful painted buildings.

BEFORE YOU GO

We can't forget to visit Caño Cristales, or the River of Five Colors, for a beautiful sight. It is usually most colorful from June to November.

What have you learned about Colombia on this trip?

Finally, we can take a trip to see the painted **tombs** at the national park in Tierradentro. These tombs are thousands of years old and have black, red, and white patterns all over them.

GLOSSARY

borders lines that show where one place ends and another begins

carnival a celebration with music, dancing, and parades

continent one of the world's seven large land masses

costumes clothes that are worn to make people look like something or someone else

indigenous originating from a particular place, often a term used for the first people in an area

jungle a thick forest in a hot place

national having to do with a country

street art paintings or drawings that are made on the sides of buildings

tombs graves, rooms, or buildings in which dead bodies are buried

weave to form by lacing together strands of material

INDEX

24